MW00881921

The True Cost of Minimum Wage

Economic Insights, Social Impacts, and the Path Forward

Penny Pincher

Copyright © 2024 by Penny Pincher

All rights reserved. No part of this publication may be reproduced, distributed, or transmitted in any form or by any means, including photocopying, recording, or other electronic or mechanical methods, without the prior written permission of the publisher, except in the case of brief quotations embodied in critical reviews and certain other noncommercial uses permitted by copyright law.

Table of Content

Introduction to Minimum Wage Policies

Imagine a small town where the early morning light paints narrow streets with a gentle, golden hue. People are just beginning their days: a baker pulling out the first trays of bread, a barista grinding coffee beans, and a cleaner, broom in hand, sweeping away yesterday's dust from a quiet storefront. These workers—essential but often unseen—embody the heartbeat of a community. For them, the minimum wage isn't merely a number on a payslip; it's a lifeline that ties their daily labour to a basic, dignified livelihood.

Minimum wage policies were conceived not just as financial tools but as moral compasses that guide economies toward a fairer society. They began as a promise from the state to the worker—a guarantee that effort and time invested in work would translate to more than just survival. This promise echoes through bustling urban centers and quiet rural landscapes alike, saying, "Your work has value, and here is the baseline that recognizes it."

Historically, minimum wage policies emerged as shields for the most vulnerable. They offered a stand against exploitation, a way to counterbalance the unchecked power employers might wield in settings where options are limited and workers lack bargaining power. The minimum wage became a mechanism to stabilize lives, reducing the risks of poverty that once ensnared workers despite their dedication and long hours.

In essence, the concept of minimum wage serves a dual role: it is both an economic instrument designed to prevent labor exploitation and a societal affirmation of fairness, saying that every working person deserves, at the very least, a basic standard of living for their efforts.

Now, imagine leaving that small town and journeying across the globe, from the neon-lit cityscape of Tokyo to the vibrant markets of Mumbai. In each place, the idea of a "minimum wage" adapts to unique cultural, political, and economic landscapes. No two countries approach it in precisely the same way, yet each reflects an underlying recognition of its power to shape lives.

In Australia, the minimum wage is reviewed and adjusted annually, ensuring that even the lowest earners keep pace with living costs in a country known for high standards of living. Picture a barista in Sydney who, like her peers across the continent, can rely on a national wage floor that matches the country's high cost of living. The review process is meticulous, a collaborative effort involving economists, policymakers, and workers' representatives who examine inflation rates, consumer price indices, and the broader economic climate before setting each year's rate.

Meanwhile, in the United States, the minimum wage landscape resembles a complex mosaic.

Federal law sets a minimum wage, yet individual states have the autonomy to establish their own, often higher rates. California's minimum wage, for instance, far exceeds the federal baseline. This approach reflects the vast diversity within the country, where the cost of living in New York City bears little resemblance to that in a rural town in Alabama. And while debates around raising the federal minimum wage remain heated, states like Washington and cities like Seattle push forward, raising their own rates to meet local demands.

In Europe, the discussion around minimum wage takes on a different tone. Countries like France have enshrined regular wage adjustments as part of their labor law, with increases automatically tied to inflation. This approach offers workers a sense of security; their wages will rise in tandem with living costs, reducing the erosion of purchasing power. Germany, relatively new to the minimum wage, introduced it only in 2015 after decades of resisting the policy. Yet, with rising public demand for fair wages, the country joined its European neighbors in setting a wage floor. In the UK, Ireland, and Spain, the rates vary but share a common goal: to lift up the lowest earners in a way that complements social support systems.

Then, there are regions where the minimum wage does not carry the same weight or coverage, such as parts of sub-Saharan Africa. In some countries, minimum wage laws apply only to formal sectors, leaving millions of workers in informal economies without protection. In Nigeria, for instance, recent efforts have seen the minimum wage raised, but implementation faces challenges, as enforcement mechanisms are often limited. Here, workers in the informal sector—domestic workers, farmers, market vendors—navigate an unregulated landscape where the minimum wage offers little, if any, support.

The global view reveals that while minimum wage policies vary, they remain a universal touchstone, a way for governments to grapple with poverty, income inequality, and workers' rights within their borders.

To understand the UK's relationship with the minimum wage, we must return to the Industrial Revolution, a period when labor was plentiful and protections were scarce. The late 19th and early 20th centuries saw harsh working conditions in factories, with long hours, low pay, and little regard for worker welfare. Voices advocating for better wages grew louder, and by 1909, the UK introduced its first wage regulation: the Trade Boards Act. This legislation established boards to set minimum wages in industries where "sweating" (a term for exploitation) was most severe, such as tailoring and box-making. The boards became early arbiters of fair pay, ensuring workers had a means to contest unjust wages.

Fast forward to the late 20th century. Amid economic shifts and mounting calls for reform, the UK finally established a comprehensive national minimum wage policy in 1998 under the Labour government. The National Minimum Wage Act laid the groundwork, setting a universal wage floor and marking a significant shift towardlabourr protection. From its initial rate, which was modest by today's standards, the minimum wage has since risen steadily, with regular adjustments to account for inflation and cost-of-living increases.

In 2016, the UK introduced the National Living Wage, a higher rate applied to workers aged 23 and above. This change acknowledged the higher costs faced by adult workers, particularly those with families. The Living Wage rate, often slightly above the minimum wage, aimed to ensure a standard that reflected the basic needs of a full-time worker living independently. The policy shift toward a "living wage" underscored a growing awareness that minimum wage alone was not enough to guarantee economic security in a high-cost society.

Today, the UK's minimum wage structure is multi-tiered, with different rates for workers under 18, apprentices, and young adults. This structure aims to balance economic realities with the goal of protecting vulnerable workers. However, debates persist about the adequacy of these rates. Advocacy groups argue that the minimum wage still falls short of a true "living wage," pushing for further increases that would bring the wage closer to the real cost of living in cities like London.

This evolution reflects the UK's journey toward a fairer wage system, shaped by changing economic conditions, societal values, and persistent advocacy for workers' rights.

Chapter 1: 2024 Minimum Wage Hike in the UK

In April 2024, the UK government announced an increase in both the National Minimum Wage and the National Living Wage, setting the stage for change that thousands of low-income workers had long awaited. This adjustment, however minor to some, feels momentous to the woman working double shifts at a cafe near Trafalgar Square, to the warehouse assistant stacking boxes in a dimly lit depot outside Birmingham, and to the barista watching her coins stretch thin in a neighborhood that seems to grow more expensive every day.

As the new rates took effect, they reflected an intricate web of decisions made months, even years, before. For workers aged 23 and over, the National Living Wage rose to £11.44 per hour, up from the previous rate of £10.42. Young adults aged 21 to 22 saw their rate inch up to £10.18, while the minimum wage for apprentices also rose, though at a lower rate. These adjustments reflect the tiers of labor in the UK, acknowledging the varied challenges faced by different age groups and roles, and aligning wages with the cost of living.

To many workers, these numbers may appear incremental. But in the rhythm of everyday life, they translate into real and tangible changes. For instance, the additional 40 pence per hour might mean a young mother working at a grocery store can afford her son's school shoes a bit sooner, or that a university student juggling part-time work and studies can manage a few more hours of rest each week. Yet for others, the increase doesn't stretch quite far enough, and the rising costs of goods and rent cast a shadow on these well-intentioned figures.

To fully appreciate the 2024 increase, one must consider the economic forces that shape the UK's financial landscape. In the past few years, the UK economy has faced pressures that many economists compare to seismic shifts. Inflation, surging energy prices, and supply chain disruptions have all contributed to rising living costs. Picture an ordinary citizen, a father, standing in the aisle of his local grocery store, where each item's price seems to tick upward weekly. The modest weekly grocery budget he once relied on now struggles to cover essentials.

Throughout 2023, inflation surged beyond what even seasoned economists had forecasted. Essentials such as food and fuel, often the highest cost burdens for low-income households, saw the steepest increases. Consequently, the real value of wages eroded, even as the job market tightened, leaving many workers feeling the effects in their monthly budgeting. In this economic environment, the minimum wage increase was not merely a routine adjustment but a necessary intervention, aimed at helping the country's lowest earners keep pace with the relentless tide of inflation.

Then there are the factors of rent and housing. In London and other major cities, rents rose dramatically, often far outpacing wage increases. Housing shortages and rising interest rates further squeezed renters, many of whom spend the bulk of their income on simply maintaining a roof over their heads. For those on minimum wage, who often find themselves sharing accommodations or forgoing essentials to meet housing costs, this squeeze felt almost inescapable.

The UK government's decision to raise the minimum wage was not made in a vacuum. It responded to these pressures with the intent to balance economic support with sustainable fiscal policy. In doing so, it sought advice from the Low Pay Commission, a body that regularly assesses the state of the workforce and the financial conditions that impact wage decisions. The commission's studies and data played a critical role in determining the extent of this year's increase, underscoring how inflation and economic hardship had left low-wage workers in a vulnerable position.

In the corridors of Westminster, discussions around minimum wage policy are steeped in a mix of pragmatism and empathy, with ministers weighing economic stability against the social imperatives of fairness and well-being. In announcing the 2024 increase, government representatives highlighted the commitment to "making work pay" for all citizens, framing the adjustment as part of a broader mission to uplift the standard of living across the UK.

For policymakers, these adjustments are more than numbers; they reflect an ongoing effort to address the economic divide that stretches across regions and social classes. Each rate increase involves the intricate calculations of economic advisors and the pressures of public expectations. Ministers took to the podium to assure citizens that the new rates are aligned with the government's mission to combat income inequality, and for some, this move is a reflection of the government's desire to safeguard the UK's workers from the worst effects of inflation and rising costs.

Yet, as with any major policy, the public response has been a blend of gratitude and criticism. On the one hand, workers' unions and advocacy groups see the increase as a step in the right direction, acknowledging that these higher rates will bring relief to thousands who have felt the weight of financial pressures. Union representatives lauded the increase, describing it as a "small victory for working-class people," though they continue to push for a minimum wage that would fully reflect a living wage, especially in high-cost areas like London.

On the other hand, small business owners have raised concerns about their ability to absorb these higher labor costs without compromising their own financial stability. A small shop owner in Brighton, for example, might face a dilemma: to raise prices or reduce staff hours in order to accommodate the increase. These employers, already struggling under the weight of high energy bills and supply costs, find themselves balancing on a knife's edge, with little room for error.

Among workers, the reaction has been varied but unmistakably charged with emotion. Many are cautiously optimistic, feeling that while the wage increase is a positive development, it falls short of the substantial raise that would bridge the gap between income and real living costs. A warehouse worker in Manchester described his feelings as "bittersweet"—grateful for the boost, yet aware that it may not fully cover the increases he's seen in rent and transportation. For him, as for many others, the minimum wage increase represents progress, but it also underscores the distance still to go.

In workplaces across the country, these changes ripple through payrolls, altering the fabric of everyday life. From a mother who carefully budgets each week to afford childcare, to a young graduate paying off loans while working a retail job, each story is touched by the shift in policy. And while government officials continue to assess future adjustments, the people affected live out the daily reality of these decisions, one shift, one payslip at a time.

Chapter 2: Real Living Wage: A Voluntary Standard

The Real Living Wage is not an official mandate; it's a promise that employers make to their workers, a commitment that says, "We value you enough to ensure you can truly live, not just survive." It's a quiet but profound shift from mere compliance with the government's minimum wage regulations to a recognition of workers' needs beyond basic survival. Developed by the Living Wage Foundation in the UK, this wage takes root in the reality of today's expenses, from housing and food to the small but essential costs that allow a person not only to exist but to participate in society.

In a quiet office in London's East End, two figures sit side by side, deep in discussion. They're representatives of the Living Wage Foundation, and their conversation is not about figures on a spreadsheet but about lives—parents who budget down to the pence, students scraping together fare for the morning commute, families trying to keep up with relentless rent hikes. For them, calculating the Real Living Wage is not a bureaucratic task but a personal one. They start by examining the costs that fill a person's day: a loaf of bread, the rising price of electricity, the ever-shifting rental market in cities like London and Manchester. The criteria for this wage are straightforward in principle yet complex in practice: it must cover the full cost of living, ensuring that those who earn it can afford life's basics in addition to enjoying some small comforts without financial distress.

Unlike the National Minimum Wage, which applies across the board by law, the Real Living Wage is a choice employers make. It's a rate that reflects the actual cost of living in the UK, calculated not merely for profit margins but for people's well-being. Currently, the Real Living Wage stands at £12.60 per hour across the UK, with a London rate of £13.85 to account for the capital's soaring costs. These numbers aren't arbitrary; they come from analyzing real expenses, from food and rent to transportation and child care. In London, where rent can swallow half a paycheck, the higher rate acknowledges a fundamental truth: it costs more to live in the city, and workers there deserve a wage that keeps pace.

Walk into the office lobby of Nationwide, one of the UK's largest building societies, and it becomes clear that their commitment to the Real Living Wage is not just a corporate policy. Employees here, from senior managers to the janitorial staff, feel the impact of a company culture that chooses to pay more than the legal minimum. Nationwide's CEO openly discusses the importance of this decision, seeing it as part of a responsibility to uplift every worker in the company. Similarly, companies like Aviva, LUSH, and KPMG have all committed to paying the Real Living Wage, making a public pledge to prioritize the well-being of their workforce over saving on wage expenses.

In the case of IKEA, the decision to adopt the Real Living Wage extended beyond frontline workers to include contracted staff like cleaners and security personnel. Imagine walking through IKEA's sprawling warehouse floors, seeing workers stocking shelves with the knowledge that their pay truly reflects their value. The company, known for its progressive employee policies, believes that paying the Real Living Wage helps create a sense of respect and loyalty among workers—a belief that is echoed by employees who feel a renewed sense of pride in their roles.

These commitments aren't made in isolation. Each year, when these companies announce their support for the Real Living Wage, they signal to others in their industry: this is a standard worth upholding. In a society where wage disparity often goes unquestioned, these employers set a benchmark that others are gradually choosing to meet, not out of obligation, but as a declaration that every employee's well-being matters.

The Real Living Wage's differentiation—£12.60 across the UK and £13.85 in London—is more than a symbolic gesture; it's a reflection of survival in one of the most expensive cities in the world. In London's East End, for instance, a young teacher's aide named Emily relies on every pound of her paycheck to cover rent, groceries, and her daily Tube fare. She spends her evenings tutoring students on the side, adding a few extra pounds each week just to meet basic needs. For her, the higher Real Living Wage rate means the difference between managing and struggling, between a chance to save and a perpetual state of financial anxiety.

Outside of London, however, the impact of the Real Living Wage shifts. In cities like Manchester or Liverpool, where living costs are notably lower, the national rate provides workers with a more sustainable income. Here, a retail worker on the Real Living Wage may actually be able to save, or at least afford a few small luxuries each month—dinners out, a cinema ticket, or a new coat for winter. These regional disparities highlight the complexities of wage policy in a country where a single rate simply cannot account for the variance in living costs from one city to the next.

In essence, the Real Living Wage acknowledges the nuance of regional economics, a nod to the reality that a worker's pound in London does not stretch as far as it might in Sheffield. But the disparity also reveals a deeper truth about inequality: that the city which drives much of the country's economy also presents its greatest cost burden to the very workers who keep it running.

Case Studies: Companies Adopting the Living Wage and Employee Impact

Picture a busy LUSH cosmetics store during the holiday rush, where the scent of handmade soaps and essential oils fills the air. Shoppers flow in and out, picking up gift-wrapped bath bombs and perfumes, greeted by a team of workers who, despite the frenetic pace, wear genuine smiles. This is no ordinary retail environment. Every staff member here, from seasonal workers to full-time employees, earns the Real Living Wage. LUSH's commitment to this wage is more than a policy; it's woven into the ethos of the company, creating a sense of purpose and respect that flows from top to bottom.

Take Rachel, for instance, a young retail worker who joined LUSH to support herself through university. Before this job, she had worked at a fast-food chain where long hours yielded little more than minimum wage, and breaks were scarce. Here, however, she feels valued. Her paycheck isn't just enough to cover rent; it allows her to manage school expenses without worry. For Rachel, the Real Living Wage means stability and the chance to focus on her studies without the cloud of financial insecurity hanging over her.

Now, shift to the corridors of KPMG, where the commitment to the Real Living Wage extends to everyone who steps through their doors. This includes contracted cleaning staff who, in many companies, often receive only the bare minimum. At KPMG, these workers are paid the Real Living Wage, a decision that aligns with the company's belief in fair treatment across all job roles. Imagine Maria, a cleaner who works the early shift, arriving at the office hours before anyone else. Her work goes unseen by most, yet it's crucial to the company's operations. With her paycheck aligned to the Real Living Wage, Maria can afford a small flat nearby, and she no longer worries about choosing between paying for utilities or groceries. Her role, often undervalued in other companies, is recognized here as an essential part of the organization's fabric.

These case studies illustrate that the Real Living Wage does more than just raise income; it changes lives. Workers describe a newfound sense of dignity, a feeling that their efforts are seen and appreciated. For companies, adopting the Real Living Wage translates into higher morale, lower turnover, and a stronger bond between employer and employee. It's a cycle of mutual respect, where both parties invest in each other, strengthening the foundations of the workplace.

And so, as the Real Living Wage continues to gain traction, it reshapes the story of work in the UK—not by mandate, but by choice, from companies that see value not just in their bottom line, but in the lives they touch.

Chapter 3: Economic and Social Impact of Minimum Wage

Picture a family in Manchester: the father works as a delivery driver for a major logistics company, the mother as a cashier at a supermarket. Both are employed full-time, and each brings home a paycheck that meets the minimum wage. Their days are spent juggling shifts and family duties, their evenings a blend of quick dinners, homework sessions with their children, and hours spent catching up on household chores. And every month, as bills stack up, their earnings—while keeping them above the poverty line—do little more than sustain a tightrope walk, stretched between necessity and insufficiency.

Minimum wage, in this scene, serves as a stabilizer, holding back the tide of poverty while still leaving the family just out of reach of real financial security. The concept of a minimum wage as a tool to reduce inequality means more than just survival; it's about closing the gap between those at the very bottom of the income ladder and the rest of society. When implemented effectively, a minimum wage helps level the playing field, giving families like this one a foothold, however small, to participate in a society that otherwise might feel out of reach.

But minimum wage doesn't operate in isolation. For every household, each pound represents an opportunity to keep up with bills or save, even if only a little. Studies have shown that higher minimum wages contribute to reducing income inequality, not only by lifting the lowest earners but by putting upward pressure on wages in roles just above the minimum. In countries like the UK, where minimum wage adjustments have taken place steadily over the years, there is tangible progress. Low-wage workers are gradually seeing income growth that, while not immediately transformative, shapes a long-term pathway toward reduced inequality and increased financial stability.

Effects on Consumer Spending and Economic Growth

Now imagine the bustling aisles of a supermarket in Birmingham, where customers mill about, filling their baskets with essentials and the occasional treat. Among them are low-wage workers from the neighborhood—restaurant servers, retail clerks, delivery drivers. They too are shoppers, carefully budgeting each pound, each decision, trying to make their earnings stretch as far as possible. For them, every extra bit of disposable income changes the experience of shopping, creating the possibility to purchase a few more items or even save a small amount.

In the economy, this pattern isn't isolated. When minimum wages increase, so does the purchasing power of low-income workers. And this effect ripples out, amplifying the flow of money across communities. A delivery driver, for instance, may spend a portion of his earnings on fuel and groceries, injecting money into local businesses. A cashier might take her family out for a meal at a neighborhood café, helping sustain jobs in the food service sector. Through this lens, minimum wage becomes not only an instrument for individual welfare but a collective force that drives demand, encouraging businesses to meet this growing purchasing power.

Economists have often pointed out that consumer spending forms the backbone of economic growth, especially in economies where the service sector is dominant. When workers at the lowest end of the pay scale earn more, they spend more—on clothes, on transportation, on basic leisure—which fuels business revenue and supports job stability. While critics argue that higher minimum wages can lead to price inflation, the net effect often results in a balanced economic stimulus, where increased consumer spending lifts demand, indirectly supporting job creation and stability in sectors that rely heavily on consumer activity.

The Role of Minimum Wage in Addressing the Cost-of-Living Crisis

Imagine a single mother in Glasgow, coming home after a double shift at a local nursing home. She works hard, her shifts demanding both physically and emotionally, but her minimum-wage paycheck often feels like a taunting reminder of her limitations. Rent, utilities, groceries—the rising cost of living in her city stretches her income thin. For her and countless others, minimum wage represents a vital part of the struggle to keep up, to hold the line against financial pressures that seem to grow heavier with each passing month.

Minimum wage adjustments directly impact people facing the ongoing cost-of-living crisis, a reality that has only intensified in recent years. The UK has seen housing prices soar, utilities skyrocket, and the price of essentials increase rapidly, making it harder for low-wage workers to afford the basics. Every time the minimum wage is raised, it serves as a buffer, albeit small, against these pressures. For many, the additional income offers the chance to afford decent housing, reliable transportation, or a bit of breathing room in their grocery budget.

For governments, raising the minimum wage is part of a broader strategy to address these economic pressures. They see it as a mechanism to counterbalance inflationary trends, ensuring that workers can keep pace with rising costs. However, it's a balancing act, as wage increases must be carefully calibrated to avoid fueling further inflation. For families facing the unyielding climb of the cost of living, a minimum wage increase is both a relief and a reminder of the ongoing struggle to maintain a foothold in an expensive economy.

Across the country, from bustling metropolises to quiet rural communities, the impact of minimum wage policies varies widely, often falling short of the ideals represented by the Real Living Wage. Imagine an office in central

London where two employees, both full-time, receive different pay due to their employers' wage policies. One earns the National Minimum Wage, while the other earns the Real Living Wage—a rate that reflects not just a basic floor for pay but a calculation of the true costs associated with living in one of the most expensive cities in the world.

The difference in their lives is striking. For the employee on minimum wage, budgeting is a constant battle; each paycheck is accounted for down to the last penny, covering necessities with little room for emergencies or leisure. Meanwhile, the employee earning the Real Living Wage has a small buffer, enough to plan, to save, to think a bit beyond the immediacy of bills. This contrast brings to light a crucial issue: while minimum wage aims to ensure basic economic stability, the Real Living Wage strives to provide a foundation for actual security and comfort.

In cities like London, where housing prices far exceed the national average, the Real Living

Wage makes a tangible difference. It considers variables that minimum wage does not, such as rent hikes, transportation costs, and even the prices of groceries, which vary significantly between regions. As more employers voluntarily adopt the Real Living Wage, they create pockets of economic resilience for their employees, reducing financial stress and contributing to a more stable, motivated workforce.

On a broader scale, the Real Living Wage also influences the conversation around what constitutes a fair wage. It sets a higher standard, pushing both private and public sectors to reconsider what it means to compensate workers adequately. As this wage gains traction, it presents a challenge to minimum wage policies, revealing gaps in coverage and adequacy that minimum wage alone cannot bridge.

Chapter 4: Minimum Wage Compliance and Enforcement in the UK

At dawn, before most people have poured their first cup of coffee, a team of inspectors from HM Revenue and Customs (HMRC) prepares for a day that will lead them across various workspaces, each one holding stories of pay, rights, and, sometimes, hidden injustice. These inspectors are part of the UK's invisible infrastructure, an entity that exists not to set wages but to ensure they are paid as legally required, protecting workers from exploitation and companies from cutting corners. For HMRC, enforcing the minimum wage is not a job but a calling to safeguard the integrity of the UK's labor market.

The inspectors move through bustling city offices, silent warehouses, and rural farms, sometimes meeting cooperative employers eager to show their compliance, and other times encountering layers of resistance that speak to the tension surrounding minimum wage laws. The inspectors' work may appear procedural, but each investigation reveals a deeper web of human stories. For workers, HMRC represents a lifeline. A barista in a high-street coffee shop, an elderly cleaner who works after hours, a young intern filling his first role—they each have rights protected by the enforcement team, even if they aren't always aware of it.

Under the Minimum Wage Act, HMRC's role in ensuring compliance is essential. Employers are legally required to maintain transparent wage records, and HMRC has the authority to demand these records without prior notice. When violations surface, they wield the power to enforce fines and demand back pay, often reaching years back, ensuring that every penny due to a worker finds its way into their pocket. Yet, beyond statistics and penalties, this work represents something bigger: a message to every worker and employer in the UK that there are boundaries, rules that ensure no one's work is undervalued.

Case Studies of Violations and Penalties

Imagine a dimly lit storeroom in a high-end restaurant, where a young waitress in a crisp white uniform hangs her apron after a long shift. She joined the establishment full of enthusiasm, her first real job since finishing school. But as weeks turned to months, her paycheck seemed smaller than expected. Confused, she approached her manager only to be told, vaguely, about "deductions" for meals and uniforms—costs she hadn't agreed to but was afraid to challenge. This waitress's story became part of an HMRC case when, following an anonymous tip, inspectors investigated and found systemic violations in the restaurant's payroll practices.

The investigation revealed that not only were deductions unlawful, but they reduced workers' wages below the legal minimum. The penalties that followed were substantial, with the restaurant facing both hefty fines and an order to repay every underpaid worker. The outcome sent ripples through the industry, a reminder that even high-profile establishments must adhere to the law. For the waitress, the investigation was transformative; her pay was corrected, her trust in her own rights restored, and her story one of justice achieved.

Another case unfolded in a small factory on the outskirts of Leeds. Here, several employees had been clocking in overtime hours without fair compensation. A factory worker named Paul, a father of three, was working twelve-hour shifts, six days a week, to provide for his family, only to find that his additional hours weren't paid in full. When HMRC's inspectors entered the scene, they discovered that the factory's payroll system had been quietly rounding down hours worked, a practice that accumulated into thousands of pounds in unpaid wages across the workforce. The factory was not only fined but also required to adjust its payroll practices to ensure transparency and fairness going forward. For Paul and his colleagues, the outcome validated their work and gave them back the dignity of fair pay.

These cases show that HMRC's role is more than administrative; it serves as a protective shield for those whose voices might otherwise go unheard. For every case resolved, there is a story of a worker who gains, at last, the pay they deserve.

New Approaches: The Geographical Compliance Approach (GCA)

On a chilly morning in the Cumbrian countryside, HMRC launched a new pilot initiative known as the Geographical Compliance Approach (GCA). Unlike traditional inspections, the GCA focused on specific regions where wage violations were suspected to be more prevalent. HMRC's teams traveled to designated areas with the intent of creating ripples, raising awareness and triggering a shift in employer practices not through punitive measures alone, but through education and outreach.

In a small town in Cumbria, local businesses—from corner shops to large construction sites—received letters from HMRC introducing the GCA. The letters outlined the minimum wage requirements, penalties for non-compliance, and offered resources for business owners to ensure they were meeting legal standards. The effect was immediate: local business owners began attending HMRC's informational sessions, asking questions, and adjusting payroll practices to align with the law.

For workers, the GCA created an unspoken assurance, a feeling that their rights were recognized and that their contributions, whether on farms, in shops, or at hotels, were being valued. The impact of GCA was twofold: it directly corrected wage violations in targeted areas while indirectly fostering a culture of compliance. Employers, knowing they were under HMRC's watchful eye, were more vigilant, and workers grew more aware of their rights. Through GCA, HMRC reminded employers that, in every corner of the UK, from large cities to rural regions, minimum wage laws applied universally.

Technology and Tools Used in Wage Compliance Monitoring

Imagine a quiet office space where data analysts pore over rows and columns on computer screens, each number and figure a potential clue. For these analysts, wage compliance isn't just about on-the-ground inspections; it's a puzzle that can often be solved through data. In recent years, HMRC has incorporated advanced technology into its wage compliance monitoring processes, using tools that bring a new level of precision to their investigations.

One such tool is data analysis software that tracks payroll trends across various industries. By analyzing payroll records en masse, HMRC can identify patterns that may signal wage violations. If a group of employers in a specific industry or region shows unusually low wage averages, it raises a flag. These flagged cases often become the focus of targeted inspections, allowing HMRC to direct its resources where they are needed most. Through this approach, technology acts as a silent watchdog, detecting irregularities before they snowball into systemic issues.

Beyond traditional methods, HMRC has begun to experiment with machine learning algorithms that can predict potential non-compliance. These algorithms process vast amounts of data, from industry payroll reports to regional economic conditions, learning to recognize risk factors that correlate with wage violations. It's a preventative measure, aiming not only to catch existing violations but to anticipate areas where non-compliance may occur. For HMRC, the goal of these technological tools is clear: to make wage compliance monitoring both faster and more accurate, protecting workers across the UK without unnecessary delays.

In recent pilot programs, these data-driven tools have proven effective. Take, for instance, the case of a retail chain with multiple branches across the UK. HMRC's data analysis revealed discrepancies in wage reporting between branches, leading to an investigation that uncovered underpayment in over a dozen locations. The company, once aware of the issue, took corrective action, adjusting wages and reimbursing affected workers. This proactive approach demonstrates the impact of technology in wage compliance, shifting enforcement from reaction to prevention.

Chapter 5: Youth and Apprenticeship Wages

Imagine a small coffee shop in the heart of Manchester, where the early morning light filters through the windows, catching the steam rising from the espresso machine. Behind the counter, a young barista named Chloe is working her first real job. At seventeen, this position represents more than just income; it's an introduction to responsibility and the rhythm of adult life. Yet, while Chloe performs the same tasks as her older colleagues—brewing coffee, ringing up sales, cleaning tables—her paycheck tells a different story. Her hourly wage is set at the youth rate, a reduced minimum wage designed for workers under the age of 18.

The youth minimum wage structure in the UK sets a different baseline for young workers, with varying rates depending on age groups. As of 2024, those under 18 earn a minimum wage lower than their adult counterparts, while apprentices, regardless of age, often start with an even lower rate. This system is based on the rationale that younger workers, typically without dependents or significant financial obligations, do not require the same wage level as adults. However, this reasoning doesn't lessen the sting for Chloe and her peers. For them, these wages shape not just their bank accounts but their relationship with work, instilling lessons in worth and contribution that they carry forward into adulthood.

The youth wage exists within a broader landscape of economic policies, designed to encourage employers to take on younger, less experienced workers. The reduced rate is intended to offset the training and support that young employees often require as they adapt to the workforce. The policy aims to make it easier for businesses to hire young people, opening doors to work experience that might otherwise remain closed.

But beneath these economic justifications lies the lived reality for young workers like Chloe. In towns and cities across the UK, youth wages are part of the story of growing up, a story in which each paycheck carries both the excitement of independence and the frustration of limitations.

Impact of Lower Youth Wages on Income and Employment

Now shift to the north, to a bustling warehouse in Sheffield, where eighteen-year-old Jayden pushes a cart loaded with packages across a dimly lit floor. He joined the warehouse team fresh out of school, driven by a desire to earn his own income and support his family. Despite his age, Jayden works long hours, lifting heavy boxes, learning the fast-paced logistics that keep the warehouse running. And yet, his paycheck—due to the youth wage rate—is only a fraction of what his older colleagues earn for the same work.

For Jayden, this lower wage means constant calculations, balancing necessities with his earnings, stretching each pound to cover both essentials and small indulgences. He dreams of saving for a car, gaining that first taste of independence, but each month brings new expenses and fresh reminders of the financial limitations he faces. For many young workers, the reduced wage is not just a number; it's a boundary that defines their aspirations and tempers their enthusiasm for work.

The impact of lower youth wages extends beyond the individual, shaping the broader landscape of youth employment. Employers, incentivized by lower wages, are more likely to hire younger workers, providing them with crucial experience in entry-level roles. This approach fosters a pipeline of young talent in industries like retail, food service, and logistics, sectors that often serve as the first step into the workforce.

However, this system also creates a dependency on low-wage, high-turnover roles that limit upward mobility for young workers. Many find themselves cycling through a series of low-paying jobs, each position building skills but offering few opportunities for advancement. As Jayden's story unfolds, it reflects the duality of youth wages: a door to opportunity that, once opened, reveals both the promise of experience and the restrictions of limited income.

Trends in Youth Employment and Economic Independence

In London's busy streets, 21-year-old Emma is juggling three part-time jobs while attending university. By day, she's a teaching assistant at a local school; by evening, she waits tables at a nearby restaurant; on weekends, she tutors students in math. Each role adds to her experience, but together, they barely cover her rent in a shared flat, let alone tuition and daily expenses. Emma's situation reflects a broader trend in youth employment across the UK: a rise in part-time, flexible work that allows young people to balance studies with income but often leaves them financially insecure.

This pattern isn't unique to Emma. Across the country, young workers are navigating a labor market that offers flexibility at the cost of stability. The rise of gig economy jobs—delivery services, freelance work, and short-term contracts—has created new pathways for youth employment, providing alternatives to traditional roles. Yet, while these jobs offer autonomy, they often lack the protections and predictability associated with full-time work. Emma's generation is one marked by independence, but that independence comes with financial risks, as fluctuating income and limited benefits make saving nearly impossible.

Economic independence for young workers remains a shifting concept. For many, the path to financial self-sufficiency is winding, shaped by a combination of wage rates, job availability, and the cost of living. Youth wages, designed to provide a stepping stone, often prove to be just that—a temporary foundation that offers initial support but requires careful navigation to reach true independence.

Chapter 6: Political Debate Around Minimum Wage Adjustments

Picture a crowded parliamentary hall, buzzing with the layered tension of a room filled with opposing ideals. Politicians sit on either side, voices low but fierce, each one armed with data, each one convinced of their position on minimum wage adjustments. On one side, proponents argue passionately for an increase, citing the skyrocketing cost of living, rising inflation, and the financial strain on low-wage workers. They remind their audience of the single parents struggling to make rent, of students who can't cover tuition while working full-time, of retired workers returning to the workforce because pensions aren't enough.

For those advocating a higher minimum wage, it's a matter of justice. They tell stories of the checkout assistant working two jobs, of the cleaner who clocks in before dawn and leaves long after the sun has set, all to bring home a paycheck that barely sustains a household. For these proponents, each figure, each rise in minimum wage, feels like a brick added to the fragile structure that shields society's most vulnerable from poverty.

But the opponents have their stories too, tales of small business owners struggling to stay afloat, of startup founders who scrape by, reinvesting every pound back into their budding businesses. They argue that raising the minimum wage imposes a burden too heavy for many small enterprises, potentially pushing them out of business. For them, it's not a question of empathy but of sustainability. They claim that too many increases could cause inflation to spiral, forcing prices up in ways that affect all consumers, including those the wage hikes intend to help.

And so, the debate churns. Proponents of higher wages insist that without meaningful increases, the minimum wage cannot serve its intended purpose. Opponents counter that while the spirit of the increase is noble, its consequences may be devastating if not tempered. In this room, each perspective holds its own emotional weight, the conflict etched in every voice, every raised eyebrow, every statistic wielded like a weapon in an ideological struggle.

Labour's Proposal for a Standardized Minimum Wage Across Ages

Step outside the debate chambers, and into the high-energy atmosphere of a Labour Party conference, where the party's new proposal takes center stage. Labour's leader stands before a packed hall, outlining a vision to establish a single, standardized minimum wage for all workers, regardless of age. As he speaks, the room falls into a hushed focus, absorbing his words, feeling the weight of this proposed shift.

In Labour's vision, young workers, from apprentices to those just entering full-time employment, would no longer face age-based wage discrepancies. They, too, would be entitled to the full minimum wage, a symbolic move that recognizes their work as equal in value to that of older colleagues. For many in attendance, this proposal feels revolutionary—a step toward dismantling the remnants of a system that undervalues youth labor. The party leader speaks of equality and fairness, emphasizing that age should not determine the worth of an hour's labor.

The audience is mixed, with young workers cheering, buoyed by the promise of financial equity, while older workers and business owners ponder the potential impacts. Some young workers share their stories: one recalls balancing two part-time jobs while studying, her hourly wage far less than her older counterparts'. For her, this proposal isn't just about money; it's about dignity, about stepping into the workforce with her contributions recognized fully. For the Labour Party, this proposal is not just policy; it's a moral stance, a pledge that no worker's age should be a determinant of value.

But as the session concludes and the applause fades, concerns linger. Business owners, particularly those in industries employing high numbers of young workers, worry aloud about the feasibility. They talk of margins and budgets stretched thin, questioning whether they can absorb this additional cost. The mood is a blend of hope and caution, the potential of a new wage structure casting both light and shadow over the hall.

Cost-of-Living Adjustments and Proposed Policy Changes

Imagine a narrow, cluttered kitchen in a small flat in London, where a father stands over a pot of pasta, the steam rising as he stirs, his mind elsewhere. He has watched food prices inch up steadily, the rent increase notice pinned to the fridge like a taunting reminder of the pressures that come from living in a major city. For him, minimum wage isn't just an abstract number; it's a lifeline that barely stretches far enough to cover the basics. When he hears news of cost-of-living adjustments being considered by Parliament, he feels a flicker of hope.

These proposed changes, under debate in Parliament, aim to link minimum wage increases to the cost of living more directly, ensuring that wages rise in tandem with inflation and essential costs. Supporters argue that without such adjustments, minimum wage becomes a hollow promise, eroded by the constant rise in living expenses. They cite studies, showing how cost-of-living adjustments in wage policies have helped stabilize income for low-wage workers, shielding them from the worst effects of economic downturns.

But not everyone agrees with this adjustment policy. In a parliamentary committee meeting, an economist outlines the potential risks, cautioning that linking wages directly to inflation could create a feedback loop, driving up both wages and prices, leaving consumers in a cycle that does little to improve purchasing power. He illustrates the dangers with a hypothetical: if wages rise to meet costs, businesses may raise prices to offset those wages, causing the cost of living to rise once more.

And yet, for the single father in the London flat, these risks seem distant. For him, the proposal is straightforward: if expenses go up, so should his pay. He doesn't think of economic cycles or inflationary feedback; he thinks of his children, their future, and his own ability to provide. For workers like him, cost-of-living adjustments represent a practical solution to a real problem, a way to ensure that wage gains are not undermined by the rising costs of the very things they're meant to cover.

The Role of Advocacy Groups and Labour Unions

In a nondescript office building, nestled between bustling high streets and corporate towers, a team of advocates from various labor unions and rights groups gathers. The walls are lined with posters—some bearing the faces of workers, others displaying slogans that speak of dignity, rights, and fair pay. This office serves as a hub for a coalition that fights tirelessly for wage reform, working to make sure the voices of workers echo within the halls of Parliament.

As the meeting unfolds, each advocate shares updates, detailing cases of wage injustice and stories of workers barely making ends meet. One speaker—a representative from a union focused on retail workers—describes a young cashier who spends her days on her feet, greeting customers with a smile while worrying about paying her electric bill. He outlines her struggle, using it to illustrate the gap between policy and reality, and to justify the union's call for a higher minimum wage.

These advocacy groups have long been a vital force in the minimum wage debate, rallying public support, staging protests, and pressuring policymakers to enact meaningful change. They meet with government officials, present research, and organize events that put real faces to the statistics—faces of baristas, cleaners, delivery drivers. For them, each policy proposal is more than a strategy; it's a lifeline for those they represent, a chance to shift the balance toward fairness and equality.

Across town, in a government office, a legislator reflects on a recent meeting with one of these advocacy groups. She recalls the workers who attended, their stories resonating long after the meeting ended. Their words reminded her that, beyond data and fiscal forecasts, there are lives at stake, shaped and molded by the outcome of each decision. For her, advocacy groups bring the human element into the legislative process, grounding the debate in the lived experiences of everyday people.

As the meeting concludes, the advocates prepare for another day's work. They know the road to fair wages is long and fraught with challenges, but they also know that change is possible. Through collective action and relentless pressure, they believe they can keep the momentum going, turning minimum wage debates into real, impactful policy shifts that benefit workers across the UK.

Chapter 7: Regional Disparities and Minimum Wage

It's a foggy morning in London, and the city is waking up with its familiar rhythm. The Underground fills with workers, commuters blending into a sea of grey and blue, briefcases, and backpacks. Among them is Dan, a young bartender who splits his week between two jobs, hustling from a café in the morning to a pub near the West End in the evening. Living in the capital has been his dream, but it's a dream that comes with a cost. Rent consumes most of his paycheck, transportation takes another slice, and food prices seem to climb with each visit to the corner shop. Each month, the same balance sheet looms over his head, a list of fixed expenses against a modest income.

Across the country, the cost of living tells a very different story. In a quiet village on the outskirts of Cornwall, Claire runs a small shop, her overheads a fraction of what Dan faces in the city. The national minimum wage—set as a standard across the UK—doesn't stretch the same way for Dan as it does for Claire. In a small town where housing is affordable, transportation costs are low, and communities have a different pace, a minimum wage job can offer a stable, if simple, living. But in London, where the average rent often rivals a monthly paycheck, the same wage barely scratches the surface of what's needed for security.

These regional disparities are woven into the UK's economic fabric, creating a minimum wage landscape that feels as diverse as the towns and cities that make up the country. In areas where the cost of living remains relatively low, minimum wage suffices, allowing workers to balance income with essential needs. But in urban centers, the same rate can leave workers like Dan on the edge, their dreams of financial security met with the constant pressure of high living costs. This contrast is not just about numbers on a payslip; it's about the very nature of life in each region, a life that minimum wage is meant to support but often struggles to sustain.

How Different Areas Are Affected by National Minimum Wage Levels

It's late in the afternoon, and in a small café in Newcastle, Emma wipes down tables, preparing for the evening crowd. Her job pays the national minimum wage, which, in this part of the North, stretches a bit farther than it would down south. Her rent is manageable, groceries are priced fairly, and though she budgets carefully, she finds that she can still set aside a bit of savings. Emma's life is not without challenges, but the cost of living here allows her a sense of stability, a feeling that her work is valued and her income sufficient.

In contrast, Dan's life in London is shaped by a different rhythm, one defined by a relentless cycle of work and expenses. Here, the national minimum wage feels less like a safety net and more like a restriction, a rate that fails to match the city's escalating cost of living. For workers in major cities, the minimum wage often seems like a starting point that doesn't adjust to the realities they face daily. Every trip to the grocery store, every ride on the Tube, and each rent payment is a reminder that the same wage set across the UK doesn't account for the region-specific pressures they experience.

This disparity echoes across other urban centers as well. In cities like Manchester and Birmingham, the cost of housing and transportation still outstrips that of rural areas, making minimum wage a tight fit for workers balancing city life's demands. For others in the countryside, the wage provides a modest but manageable existence, allowing them to cover costs without the persistent stress of urban living expenses. The national minimum wage, while providing a unifying standard, reveals its limitations when stretched across regions that demand very different levels of financial commitment from their residents.

Imagine London, a sprawling metropolis where everything seems to pulse with a frenetic energy. In a borough like Camden, young professionals, artists, and service workers fill the streets, their lives bound by the city's high pace and high costs. Dan, the bartender, is one of them. Each shift he works, each paycheck he receives, speaks to the paradox of London life: the opportunity and the cost. For Dan, every pound earned is a pound already spent, the margin for savings nearly non-existent. In London, the minimum wage feels like a tightrope walk, balanced precariously between ambition and survival, the city's allure shadowed by its expense.

Contrast this with Belfast, where the streets are quieter, the atmosphere more relaxed, and the cost of living relatively lower. Here, minimum wage workers like Liam, who works in a warehouse, find that their income goes further. Rent is affordable, public transportation reliable, and the daily expenses that eat away at Dan's paycheck seem gentler here. For Liam, the national minimum wage means stability, a foundation that allows him to consider his future with a measure of security. The same wage that Dan fights to stretch in London provides Liam with a modest but steady living, allowing him the breathing room that his urban counterparts often lack.

Now, travel south to Cornwall, where the coastline curves around small towns filled with seasonal workers, many of whom depend on minimum wage jobs in tourism. Here, Sarah works in a hotel, her pay dependent on the ebb and flow of visitors who fill the region each summer. Her income fluctuates, influenced by seasonal demand, yet the lower cost of living in the South West allows her to manage with relative ease. For Sarah, the wage provides what she needs, a wage that aligns with the town's quieter lifestyle, its lower housing costs, and the pace of life shaped by the sea's rhythm.

These case studies reveal a landscape in which the national minimum wage feels both uniform and uneven, its effects shaped by the unique characteristics of each region. In London, the wage feels stretched thin, a baseline that struggles to keep up with the city's towering expenses. In Northern Ireland, it offers stability, a wage that sustains and supports workers in a region with different demands. In Cornwall, it's a seasonal lifeline, enough to support a way of life that reflects the area's smaller scale and slower pace.

Across each of these regions, the national minimum wage reveals its strengths and its limitations. It unifies, providing a standard that all workers can rely on, yet it also divides, highlighting the gaps between what a wage can offer and what life truly costs in different parts of the UK. For workers like Dan, Liam, and Sarah, the minimum wage isn't just a policy; it's a reality that defines the rhythm, the challenges, and the possibilities of their lives.

Chapter 8: Comparative Analysis: Minimum Wage Policies Worldwide

Imagine the sprawling coastlines of Australia, where cities like Sydney and Melbourne pulse with energy against a backdrop of endless sky and sea. In this part of the world, minimum wage isn't just a figure but a promise that allows workers to hold onto a sense of security. Australia's minimum wage is among the highest globally, set at AUD $23.23 per hour as of 2024, a rate adjusted annually by the Fair Work Commission. This wage reflects the cost of living in an economy where prices are steep but balanced by strong protections for workers. Here, every year, economists, labor representatives, and government officials sit down to review and debate the national wage floor, weighing inflation, industry pressures, and workers' welfare.

Picture a bustling café near Bondi Beach, where a barista named Liam greets the morning crowd, the steady hum of coffee machines punctuating the start of each day. For Liam, the minimum wage allows him not just to meet his basic needs but to set aside a modest amount, a buffer against the unexpected. He doesn't worry about being squeezed out by rent or basic expenses; his pay reflects a fair balance, a wage that aligns with the costs that life in Sydney demands. In Australia, this alignment between wages and costs isn't accidental; it's part of a national commitment to a fair standard, one that assures workers like Liam of a financial foundation that doesn't erode with each economic shift.

Travel a bit further southeast, and you'll reach New Zealand, where the minimum wage also stands as a pillar of labor rights. As of 2024, the minimum wage here is NZD $22.70, a rate similarly recalibrated each year in line with inflation and economic conditions. New Zealand's approach to minimum wage shares much with Australia's, grounded in the understanding that a wage must not just protect against poverty but enable a modest standard of living. For a young worker in Auckland, for instance, this wage makes the difference between struggling and stability, allowing him to keep up with rent, food, and transportation without the relentless pressure of financial insecurity.

Both Australia and New Zealand have developed a system in which the minimum wage serves as a bedrock, built to sustain workers and uphold a quality of life that reflects the ideals of equity embedded in each country's labor laws. Their high minimum wages don't just reflect a high cost of living but embody a shared belief that workers deserve a wage they can rely on, one that evolves with the economy, assuring every person who clocks in that their time has inherent worth.

Lessons from U.S. State-Based Wage Variations

Now cross the Pacific and arrive in the United States, where minimum wage is far from a uniform standard. Instead, it's a patchwork quilt of state policies, each one setting its own rate in response to local cost demands, political leanings, and economic pressures. At the federal level, the minimum wage stands at $7.25, unchanged since 2009, and is one of the lowest minimum wages among developed nations. But the states themselves tell a different story, creating a mosaic of wage rates that range from the federal baseline in states like Georgia to over $15 per hour in areas like California and New York City.

Imagine a bustling coffee shop in downtown Seattle, where workers earn $18.69 per hour, the highest state-mandated minimum wage in the country. For Ethan, a part-time student who works shifts between his college classes, this wage makes it possible to pay for rent in a city known for its high costs, as well as tuition and day-to-day expenses. Seattle's wage policy, higher than both the federal rate and most state rates, is part of an intentional response to the city's elevated cost of living, ensuring that even in an expensive urban environment, workers like Ethan have a shot at financial balance.

Contrast this with a similar coffee shop across the country in Atlanta, Georgia, where minimum wage workers often earn only the federal rate. For Ashley, who works full-time in the service industry, the difference between $7.25 and Seattle's $18.69 is stark. Her wage covers only the essentials, leaving her little room for anything beyond survival. Rent alone consumes much of her paycheck, forcing her to pick up extra shifts just to make ends meet. In states that rely on the federal minimum, workers face a reality that feels worlds away from the security that workers in higher-wage states experience.

In the United States, this variation has generated a national dialogue about wage equity, as advocates push for a higher federal rate that could bridge the gap between low- and high-wage states. Each state's policy reflects a complex interplay of economics and politics, creating a landscape where a worker's quality of life is as much a product of geography as it is of employment. This patchwork system, though deeply rooted in America's federalist structure, reveals the challenges of achieving a fair and consistent standard in a country where the cost of living and political perspectives are anything but uniform.

European Union Minimum Wage Policies: Harmonization Efforts

Imagine crossing into Europe, a continent where the minimum wage isn't just a policy but a political endeavor. Here, each country's minimum wage tells a story of its own, shaped by the intricacies of national economies, regional inflation, and cultural expectations. From France's "Salaire Minimum Interprofessionnel de Croissance" (SMIC) to Germany's "Mindestlohn," each rate speaks to an attempt to balance workers' rights with economic pragmatism.

In France, the minimum wage has long been a core pillar of the country's labor system. The SMIC, as it's commonly called, is not just set; it's adjusted each January, linked to inflation and average wage increases. The French government sees it as more than a number—it's a reflection of national values. A baker in Marseille, for example, knows that each year's SMIC increase ensures her wage keeps pace with the country's economic shifts, shielding her from the pressures of rising costs. For her, the minimum wage is more than a lifeline; it's a safeguard that evolves with the times, adapting to keep her afloat.

Germany's journey to a minimum wage took longer, finally implementing a federal rate in 2015 after years of opposition and debate. Today, that rate is periodically adjusted, a calculated compromise between the needs of workers and the concerns of industry leaders. A retail worker in Berlin, benefiting from the national wage floor, feels the impact of this policy daily, her income sufficient to cover rent, food, and a few modest pleasures. Germany's late adoption of a minimum wage reflects a broader European tension between harmonization and autonomy, as each nation grapples with aligning domestic policies with EU-wide goals.

The European Union itself faces the challenge of harmonizing minimum wages across its member states, balancing the disparities that arise from different economic realities. The EU's efforts to develop a directive that would establish minimum wage frameworks across the bloc reflects this ambition, aiming to reduce inequality while respecting national sovereignty. In lower-wage countries like Bulgaria or Romania, the gap between minimum wages and cost of living remains wide, and workers often look toward the higher rates in countries like France and Germany with a sense of aspiration, if not frustration.

Chapter 9: Minimum Wage and Inflation: A Balancing Act

Imagine a bustling supermarket on the edge of Manchester. It's late afternoon, and Sarah, a single mother working as a cashier, stands at her register, scanning items and chatting with customers as they shuffle by. She smiles as she hands back change, but there's a faint line of worry creased on her forehead. Sarah's monthly budget is a delicate balance of necessities, but every pound counts, and lately, it feels like her paycheck stretches less and less. The last time her wage increased, she felt a bit of relief—her rent and food bills seemed manageable. But recently, prices for groceries, fuel, and utilities have crept higher, shrinking her paycheck in ways that make the wage increase feel like a distant memory.

For Sarah, and many others like her, inflation is a silent force that seems to move in tandem with wages, erasing the gains of each increase over time. But beneath this surface is a complex relationship, one that ties together wage policies, economic stability, and the power of purchasing. In economic terms, inflation measures the rate at which prices for goods and services rise, eroding purchasing power. When wages rise, it can be a lifeline for low-income workers like Sarah, helping them manage the increasing costs of essentials. However, wage increases alone can trigger a rise in prices if not balanced carefully—a cycle where wages chase prices, and prices chase wages, with workers caught in the middle.

This balancing act between wages and inflation is no mere calculation. It is a struggle that lives in every household and every paycheck, affecting the lives of workers and families across the country. When wages increase, particularly at a minimum level, there's a ripple effect that reaches into every corner of the economy. Employers face higher labor costs, which they may offset by raising prices on goods and services. This, in turn, impacts consumers, including the very workers whose wages have been raised. For policymakers, finding the balance is like walking a tightrope, each step heavy with the weight of economic consequences and the responsibility to protect those most vulnerable to the shifting tides of inflation.

How Inflation Affects Real Wage Value

In the small flat she shares with her two children, Sarah calculates her monthly expenses down to the last pound. Her rent has increased by £50 since the start of the year, and her electricity bill went up too. Every trip to the grocery store reveals higher prices on basic items—milk, bread, pasta. The wage increase she received a few months ago feels like it's already been swallowed whole by these rising costs. Her real wage, in effect, is shrinking, even if her hourly pay hasn't changed.

Real wage value refers to the actual purchasing power of a worker's earnings after accounting for inflation. For Sarah, the rise in the minimum wage gave her a fleeting sense of relief, but as inflation outpaces this gain, her real income declines. While her nominal wage—the number on her payslip—remains steady, her purchasing power, or what her income can actually buy, weakens. Each pound buys less than it did before, transforming small changes in price into weighty shifts in lifestyle.

The effects of this erosion are felt most acutely by workers at the minimum wage level. For Sarah, who already budgets tightly, a small increase in rent or utilities has a significant impact, leaving her with fewer choices and more compromises. This is the paradox of wage increases in an inflationary economy: a nominal rise in income feels significant at first but quickly diminishes in value as prices climb. For policymakers, the challenge is clear but complex—how to increase wages without accelerating inflation, and how to shield workers from the relentless rise in costs that eats away at the gains they work so hard to achieve.

For Sarah and her colleagues, each wage increase brings a fresh wave of hope, only to be met by the reality of diminishing returns. The more prices rise, the less each wage increase can do to ease the burden of daily life. It's a cycle that keeps workers like Sarah on the edge, striving for stability but finding it elusive in an economy that seems to always be a step ahead of them.

Strategies for Protecting Workers' Wages Against Rising Costs

In a conference room in Westminster, a group of policymakers, economists, and labor representatives gather, each one bringing perspectives from across the economic landscape. They're here to discuss strategies for protecting workers from inflation's corrosive effects, to explore ways in which wage policies can truly support those they're meant to help. It's a room charged with urgency, each voice carrying the weight of real-world consequences for workers like Sarah, for whom even a few pence per hour could mean the difference between staying afloat and struggling.

One proposal centers around cost-of-living adjustments (COLA), an approach that links wage increases directly to inflation. The idea is simple: if prices rise, so should wages, ensuring that workers maintain their purchasing power over time. But the debate is far from straightforward. Critics of COLA argue that automatic wage adjustments can create a cycle of inflationary pressure, where prices and wages fuel each other's rise. Supporters, however, believe that without such adjustments, minimum wage increases fail to keep pace with the reality of workers' lives, leaving them vulnerable to every economic shift.

Another approach discussed is targeted subsidies for essential goods and services. Rather than raising wages across the board, the government could focus on stabilizing the prices of key expenses—housing, utilities, transportation. By capping rent increases or providing subsidies for energy costs, policymakers could indirectly boost real wage value without triggering inflationary cycles. The room is split; some believe this approach addresses the root issues, while others argue that it's only a temporary fix, one that doesn't address the broader need for equitable wage policies.

Meanwhile, labor unions advocate for stronger wage floors, with regular adjustments to the minimum wage that account for both inflation and productivity. For union leaders, the solution lies in fair, predictable wage increases that give workers a chance to plan, save, and live without the fear that their income will be undercut by rising prices. They cite case studies from countries like Australia, where annual minimum wage adjustments have managed to balance economic growth with inflation control, providing a model of stability that the UK could follow.

In the end, there are no easy answers, no single strategy that will solve the complex relationship between wages and inflation. But for workers like Sarah, each proposal offers a glimmer of possibility, a hope that, perhaps, the next wage increase will be more than a fleeting reprieve. For now, she does what she can, making each pound count, adjusting to the shifting costs of a world that seems to always move faster than her paycheck.

Chapter 10: Future of Minimum Wage in the UK

The setting sun casts a golden hue over Westminster, where policymakers gather in a quiet boardroom to discuss the trajectory of the UK's minimum wage. In this room, discussions are rooted in numbers, predictions, and projections. But beyond the figures are the lives of millions of workers whose futures hinge on these decisions. Among the projections, there's cautious optimism, tempered by the complexities of an economy in flux.

The National Living Wage (NLW), set by the government for workers aged 23 and older, and the Real Living Wage (RLW), determined by the Living Wage Foundation and voluntarily adopted by some employers, both sit at the heart of this discussion. Looking ahead, experts predict that the NLW could reach £11.67 per hour by 2025, a reflection of current inflationary trends and a commitment to ensure that wages align more closely with the cost of living. For the RLW, which currently sits at £12.60 outside London and £13.85 within the city, the Living Wage Foundation's goal is to reach parity with the true cost of living across all regions.

In the boardroom, every estimate is weighed against a backdrop of potential economic shifts. Some believe that the NLW will need to increase annually by at least 5-6% to keep pace with inflation and offer workers a wage that reflects the realities of life in an increasingly costly UK. For low-wage earners, each increase represents a small but essential step toward financial stability, a chance to finally feel secure in their ability to cover rent, food, and basic needs.

Outside the boardroom, workers like Maria, a cleaner in Birmingham, follow these updates closely. Each new projection brings with it a mixture of hope and uncertainty. For Maria, the wage increases of the past few years have helped her make rent without constant anxiety, allowing her to save a little each month for emergencies.

However, she knows the effect of these raises can be fleeting if prices continue to climb. The future of minimum wage is more than an economic concept to her—it's a promise that her work will always allow her to keep her footing, that she won't be left behind as costs rise.

As the projections become more ambitious, Maria and workers like her are filled with cautious optimism. They know that even as the numbers rise, these predictions remain tethered to the unpredictable rhythms of the economy, a future in which each figure represents not just an income but a vision of stability and security for those who need it most.

Long-Term Policy Proposals and Government Goals

In a quieter part of Westminster, a coalition of policy advisers, economists, and labour advocates gather, their discussion turning to the long-term vision for minimum wage policy in the UK. The conversation is animated, focused on bold ideas and forward-thinking proposals.

Long-term policy changes, they agree, should not only support the cost of living but also enable growth, providing a genuine path to financial independence for all workers.

At the heart of these discussions are proposals to link minimum wage increases directly to national productivity. The concept is simple: as the economy grows and productivity improves, so too should the minimum wage. For supporters, this approach ensures that workers benefit from economic prosperity, directly tying wage growth to the health of the economy. It is a policy approach that signals a shift from reactive to proactive, where workers are guaranteed fair compensation in line with the UK's economic performance.

Another proposal on the table involves extending the scope of the NLW to younger workers, bridging the age gap and ensuring that all adults, regardless of age, receive a wage that reflects their contribution to the workforce. Currently, younger workers face lower wage rates, a structure that some policymakers argue fails to recognize the full value of their work. The proposal to standardize wages across age groups reflects a shift towards equity, challenging the assumption that young workers' contributions are less valuable.

As the policymakers exchange ideas, there is an awareness of the stakes involved. They talk of the larger goals: to reduce poverty, support families, and create a foundation where minimum wage can truly support a dignified life. These proposals represent more than policy adjustments; they are a vision for a fairer future, one where the minimum wage is not a floor but a stepping stone, enabling workers to move forward with confidence.

For workers like Tom, a young warehouse employee in Glasgow, these long-term goals are a glimpse of possibility. He dreams of earning a wage that reflects his hard work, a wage that allows him to look beyond the daily grind toward a future where he can plan, save, and thrive. For Tom, each policy proposal represents a promise that his work and his youth won't be barriers to financial independence, but building blocks to a stable and hopeful future.

Impact of Automation and Technological Change on Wage Needs

Picture the early hours of a factory in Manchester, where machines hum to life in a steady rhythm, producing goods with precision and speed. Over the years, automation has transformed this factory, gradually replacing roles that once required teams of workers. Today, only a few employees monitor the machines, their tasks shifting from manual labor to oversight and maintenance. For workers like Jane, who has spent years in this factory, these changes are a double-edged sword—on one hand, they've streamlined production and created safer, more efficient work environments; on the other, they've reduced the need for hands-on roles, changing the very nature of work in ways that directly impact minimum wage needs.

Automation's rise across industries like manufacturing, retail, and food service has sparked new discussions around wage policies. In sectors where machines take on repetitive tasks, human roles are evolving, shifting towards positions that require technical skills, oversight, and adaptability. For workers without these skills, the risk of displacement looms, creating a pressing need for retraining and education programs to support those impacted by technological change.

For policymakers, the question becomes clear: as automation reduces the need for traditional roles, how can minimum wage policies evolve to reflect the changing landscape of work? One idea being explored is the concept of a "digital wage"—a rate that considers the technical demands of modern roles, ensuring that workers involved in monitoring and maintaining automated systems receive compensation that reflects their skills. Another approach involves increasing investment in vocational training, creating pathways for workers to transition into new roles within automated industries, ensuring that minimum wage remains relevant in a future shaped by technology.

Outside the factory, Jane reflects on the shifts she has witnessed over the years. Automation has made her role more specialized, and with that specialization, she feels the need for wages that reflect the expertise her job now requires. She dreams of a future where technological change doesn't leave workers behind but empowers them to grow and adapt, where the minimum wage rises not just to meet cost-of-living demands but to recognize the evolving nature of work itself.

These visions—predictions for wage increases, long-term policy goals, and adaptations to technological change—are more than numbers and ideas. For workers across the UK, they are glimpses into a future where minimum wage is a dynamic force, evolving alongside the economy and technology, a promise that wages will keep pace not just with costs but with the realities of a changing world.

Chapter 11: Minimum Wage in Practice: Real-World Perspectives

In the early hours before dawn, the city's quiet is broken only by the distant hum of traffic and the soft buzz of neon lights in shop windows. In a small kitchen on the outskirts of Manchester, Maria tightens the laces on her worn sneakers, preparing for a long day of cleaning work. It's still dark outside, but she's used to it by now. This early shift is one of two jobs she juggles to make ends meet, each paycheck only just covering the bills. Maria sits for a brief moment, sipping her coffee as she mentally maps out her day: eight hours of work, a commute that eats up another hour each way, and then back home to her two young children.

"Every pound counts," she says quietly, her voice tinged with the exhaustion of years spent walking this tightrope between bills and paychecks. Her job, she explains, pays the minimum wage. It's a sum that covers necessities but leaves little room for unexpected expenses, like last winter when her son needed a new coat or when the heating bill spiked during a particularly cold snap. Maria's days are measured in minutes, in coins, in hopes that the next paycheck will offer even a small measure of relief.

For workers like Maria, the minimum wage is more than just a number on a payslip. It's a threshold that separates stability from struggle. She dreams of a future where her wage increases just enough to allow a little extra—to buy a birthday present without having to skimp on groceries or to take a day off without the worry of lost income.

Then there's Jamal, a young man working as a stocker in a supermarket in Birmingham. He took the job right after finishing school, hoping to save up for a university degree someday. "It's not easy," he says with a wry smile, adjusting his cap and glancing around the store. "You have to be smart with your money." For Jamal, the minimum wage offers a taste of independence, but it comes with limitations. Every night, he returns home with tired muscles, aware that each paycheck brings him a step closer to his goal but never quite fast enough.

Jamal's story is one of hope, tempered by reality. He dreams of studying engineering, of one day having a career that brings both fulfillment and financial security. But with his current wage, the path is long and steep. For now, he saves in small increments, making sacrifices where he can, his aspirations bound by the limits of his paycheck. Both Maria and Jamal embody the resilience of minimum wage workers, their challenges and dreams underscoring the vast distance between necessity and aspiration.

Employer Perspectives on Wage Increases and Business Viability

Across town, in the bustling business district of London, Tom stands in his modest, well-organized restaurant kitchen, hands on his hips, watching as his team prepares for the lunchtime rush. Tom is a small business owner, managing a team of ten, many of whom rely on minimum wage income to support their families. As he watches his team—dishwashers, servers, cooks—each moving with practiced efficiency, he feels a familiar knot of anxiety tighten in his chest. He knows the hard work they put in, and he wishes he could pay them more, but the numbers are what they are.

"Margins are thin in this industry," he explains, glancing over at the spreadsheets on his desk, which tell a story of their own: rising costs of ingredients, rent, utilities. Tom's dream was to open a restaurant that felt like a second home for his team and his customers alike. But every year, the prospect of minimum wage increases brings with it the need to recalibrate, to adjust prices, or sometimes, to make difficult staffing decisions. It's a constant balancing act between fairness and financial viability.

Tom isn't opposed to minimum wage increases; he supports them in principle, understanding that his employees deserve a wage that reflects their hard work and dedication. But each increase means he must adjust somewhere else, and often it feels as though he's just breaking even. For him, wage policy isn't abstract—it's a daily reality, one that affects his livelihood and his employees' stability.

On the other side of the spectrum is Claire, a manager for a nationwide retail chain. For her, wage increases are managed by the corporate office, and she sees them differently. "We adjust our budgets, maybe trim back on hours or look for efficiencies," she explains, noting that the company has systems in place to absorb these adjustments. But even so, Claire empathizes with smaller businesses that may not have the resources to adapt as easily. As she reflects on the upcoming wage increase, she wonders how it will play out for workers who have fewer hours as a result, their weekly earnings impacted in ways that a simple pay increase might not immediately solve.

For employers like Tom and Claire, wage policies are deeply personal. Each pay raise, each new policy, is a balancing act between providing fair compensation and keeping their businesses viable. It's a delicate line they walk, one that reveals both the promise and the pressure of maintaining a workforce in an evolving economic landscape.

The Social Responsibility Perspective of Large Corporations

In a sleek office high above the city, Anna sits in front of a conference table scattered with reports. She's part of the corporate social responsibility team for a major corporation, and today's discussion centers around the company's commitment to paying the Real Living Wage to all employees, including contracted staff. For Anna, this isn't just a policy—it's a promise that defines the company's relationship with its workforce. As she flips through the documents, her mind drifts to the stories she's heard from workers in their retail stores and warehouses, stories of what a fair wage means to them.

For Anna's company, paying the Real Living Wage isn't just about aligning with legal standards; it's about leading by example in an industry often scrutinized for wage practices. The decision was a bold one, met with mixed reactions from stakeholders concerned about costs. But for Anna, the impact of this policy is clear. During a recent site visit, she spoke with Oliver, a warehouse worker who had been with the company for years. When the Real Living Wage policy was implemented, Oliver's pay increased enough to allow him to move out of a shared flat into a place of his own. "It's given me my dignity," he told her, his eyes reflecting a mixture of pride and relief.

Stories like Oliver's remind Anna why her work matters. For large corporations, wage policy isn't just an economic decision; it's a statement of values. By adopting the Real Living Wage, Anna's company sends a message to its employees, its customers, and its competitors: that the work people do is valued and that a commitment to fair pay is part of the company's identity.

Not all large corporations have followed suit, however. Some remain reluctant to adopt higher wages, citing concerns over shareholder expectations and competitive pressures. Yet, for Anna and others in her field, the shift toward socially responsible wage practices feels inevitable. Every story from employees like Oliver, every acknowledgment of the difference a fair wage can make, strengthens the case for a future where corporations lead not just in profit but in purpose.

As the meeting concludes, Anna feels a sense of accomplishment. She knows there's still work to be done, still questions to answer, but each step forward in the commitment to fair wages brings her company closer to the vision she believes in—a vision where success is measured not just in numbers but in the well-being of every person who makes the company thrive.

Conclusion: Minimum Wage as a Social and Economic Tool

The story of minimum wage, woven through the lives of workers, employers, policymakers, and advocates, is a powerful narrative of resilience, hope, and ambition. It is the narrative of Maria, the cleaner in Manchester who watches every pound and dreams of the day her wage can offer a sense of stability beyond survival. It is also the journey of small business owners like Tom, caught between paying their employees a fair wage and sustaining their business, a delicate balance that shapes their decisions and their livelihoods. Each person's experience reveals an essential truth: minimum wage is far more than a policy. It's a social commitment that echoes through every corner of life, from paychecks and price tags to aspirations and anxieties.

The minimum wage's role in reducing inequality, stimulating consumer spending, and lifting families out of poverty is clear, but so too are its limitations in an ever-changing economy. Through examining real-world stories and varied global practices, we see that a one-size-fits-all approach does not fully capture the diverse needs and challenges of different regions, industries, and demographics. The disparity between minimum wage levels in regions like London and Cornwall, or the differences between countries like Australia and the U.S., illustrates how minimum wage must evolve to truly serve those it's designed to protect.

Each discussion, policy shift, and wage adjustment in the minimum wage journey underlines an ongoing evolution. The takeaway is clear: minimum wage, when thoughtfully designed and adjusted, can serve as a bridge from necessity to stability, a means of bringing social justice into the financial lives of workers across the socioeconomic spectrum.

The Evolving Role of Minimum Wage in Economic Policy

As we turn toward the future, the role of minimum wage in economic policy emerges not just as a regulatory tool, but as a dynamic force in the larger conversation of economic equality and growth. Imagine a crowded legislative chamber, where policymakers debate the next series of minimum wage reforms. They discuss economic reports, inflation rates, and the stories of workers whose paychecks define the line between security and scarcity. The air hums with urgency, as each voice in the room seeks to shape the evolving landscape of wage policies that will impact millions.

The minimum wage, once seen primarily as a means of ensuring fair compensation for entry-level work, now embodies a broader purpose. It has become a tool for shaping economic health, for closing income gaps, and for addressing the real-world needs of a labor force that spans diverse ages, skills, and industries. The question is no longer just about how much a worker earns, but about how wages affect broader goals, such as consumer spending, economic growth, and the reduction of poverty.

In recent years, countries around the world have seen how targeted minimum wage policies can stimulate local economies, encourage employment, and foster a more equitable distribution of wealth. Policymakers recognize that minimum wage is not static; it must be flexible enough to respond to inflation, regional disparities, and changes in technology and job structures. And as automation redefines labor, the minimum wage will need to adapt further, ensuring that workers in new industries, and those displaced by technological advances, are protected.

For policymakers, the role of minimum wage in economic policy is evolving into a symbol of a larger goal: to build a society where every worker, regardless of job or background, can earn a living that reflects the dignity of their labor. This shift marks a new chapter in the story of minimum wage—one where economic policy, social equity, and individual welfare converge, each goal reinforcing the others.

Future Directions for Fair Wages and Economic Equality

In a quiet café, Maria sits at a table, scrolling through her phone as she reads an article about proposed minimum wage increases. She sees mentions of "living wages," "cost-of-living adjustments," and "income equality." Each phrase resonates with her, a glimpse into a future where wages not only keep up with expenses but provide a foundation for security and dignity. For Maria and workers like her, the future of minimum wage is not just a policy debate; it's a hope for change that will transform their lives, allowing them to dream of a life beyond survival.

Looking forward, there are several pathways for realizing fair wages and promoting economic equality. First, many experts advocate for the adoption of a Real Living Wage that reflects true living costs, adjusted annually and regionally to account for the disparities in housing, transportation, and basic goods. This approach, already adopted voluntarily by some companies, could set a new standard, one that transcends the limitations of the traditional minimum wage. By linking wages to the actual cost of living, the Real Living Wage could become a cornerstone of wage policy, ensuring that every worker earns enough to meet life's fundamental needs.

Another path forward involves tying minimum wage to productivity and economic growth. Imagine a world where, as the economy prospers, so too do the workers who contribute to it. Such a model would mean that workers share in the benefits of national growth, creating a direct relationship between economic progress and personal income. This approach, advocated by some policymakers and economists, suggests that fair wages can drive economic prosperity, creating a positive cycle where higher wages lead to increased spending, which in turn stimulates business and employment growth.

There is also a growing call for comprehensive benefits programs that supplement wages, particularly in the face of automation and the gig economy's rise. For Maria, Jamal, and countless others, access to affordable healthcare, education, and retirement benefits is as critical as wage increases. By building a system where wages are supported by a network of social benefits, policymakers can create a safety net that bolsters economic equality, ensuring that workers are protected from the financial instability that often accompanies low-wage employment.

As the discussion around minimum wage moves into the future, the vision becomes clear: minimum wage is no longer just a floor; it's a foundation on which workers can build a stable, dignified life. Through fair wage policies, living wage standards, and social support systems, the future promises a world where wages reflect the true value of labor, where workers share in economic prosperity, and where every paycheck is a step toward not just survival, but a life well-lived.

The future of minimum wage is a beacon for those who labor in the shadows of economic disparity. It is a reminder that, through thoughtful policy and collective will, the journey from minimum wage to living wage is possible, a path that leads to fairness, dignity, and the hope for a brighter, more inclusive world.

Made in the USA
Columbia, SC
27 November 2024

47782738R00063